Discovering *ART*

Comic Book Art

Hal Marcovitz

ReferencePoint Press®

San Diego, CA

© 2016 ReferencePoint Press, Inc.
Printed in the United States

For more information, contact:
ReferencePoint Press, Inc.
PO Box 27779
San Diego, CA 92198
www.ReferencePointPress.com

LIBRARY OF CONGRESS CATALOGING-IN-PUBLICATION DATA

Marcovitz, Hal, author.
  Comic book art / By Hal Marcovitz.
    pages cm. -- (Discovering art)
  Includes bibliographical references and index.
  ISBN 978-1-60152-944-2 (hardback) -- ISBN 1-60152-944-9 (hardback) 1. Comic books, strips, etc.--History and criticism--Juvenile literature. I. Title.
  PN6714.M33   2016
  741.5'9--dc23
                                                                    2015030315

Contents

The Enduring Art of the Comic Book

Avengers: Age of Ultron was a major blockbuster movie of 2015. The film told the story of a battle between a team of superheroes and an evil robot intent on wiping out all human life on earth. The film earned some $500 million at the box office in America and nearly $1 billion more worldwide. Said *Variety* magazine film critic Scott Foundas, "*Avengers: Age of Ultron* [is] a super-sized spandex soap opera that's heavy on catastrophic action but surprisingly light on its feet, and rich in human-scale emotion."[1]

Adding to the film's appeal is the state-of-the-art computer-generated imagery, which helped illustrate the awesome powers of the characters: Iron Man, Hulk, Captain America, Thor, and others. Thanks to twenty-first-century special effects, audiences saw the characters defy gravity, smash through brick walls, run at supersonic speeds, toss automobiles like baseballs, and move objects with the power of the mind.

These characters made their first appearances in popular culture in a much more modest medium: the comic book. When Captain America was first introduced to readers in the 1940s, the star-spangled superhero made his debut in a publication that was hand drawn, printed on cheap paper, and sold mostly to young people for no more than a dime. As such, comic books were long derided by critics as something less than art. Says Roger Sabin, a professor at Central Saint Martin's College of Art and Design in London, "Throughout their history they have been perceived as intrinsically 'commercial,' mass-produced for a lowest-common-denominator audience, and therefore automatically outside notions of artistic credibility."[2]

Sophisticated Art

But comic books have endured into the twenty-first century, and the characters and stories they have spawned are familiar to millions of fans—not only because their popularity has been enhanced by Hollywood films but because readers remain dedicated to the art of the comic book. According to the website Comichron, which tracks comic book circulation in North America, readers spent $870 million on print versions of comic books in 2013, an increase of $65 million over 2012 sales. Also, digital versions of comic books totaled $90 million in 2013, a $20 million increase over the previous year's digital sales. Moreover, those statistics do not reflect sales of graphic novels—essentially, book-length versions of comic books. In 2014 the website ICv2 reported graphic novel sales at $415 million—a 4 percent increase over 2013 sales. Says Gus Lubin, the executive editor of the website Business Insider,

Words in Context

spandex
Synthetic fiber with an elasticity that makes it ideal for skintight exercise garments as well as costumes favored by superheroes.

> As much as the movies and technology are helping the [comic book] industry . . . even more credit should go to comic book creators. Most comics are simply better these days—and that's my personal opinion, but it's also a popular one. Comic books have become far more sophisticated since their debut last century. . . .
>
> Comics are often better than movies about the same characters, which makes sense when you think about it. Hundred-million-dollar movies are designed to reach the widest possible audience while also setting up sequels and spinoffs, which can result in something bland. Comics can meet the vision of a writer and a small team of artists with far fewer limits and nothing more at risk than cancelation.[3]

The flashy superhero characters in the 2015 movie *Avengers: Age of Ultron* (pictured) made their first public appearance decades ago in the decidedly low-tech medium of comic books. As an art form, comic books have come a long way.

No Longer Disposable Entertainment

Whereas sales figures may reflect the enduring popularity of comic books, it can also be said that by the twenty-first century, the comic book has finally been accepted as a legitimate form of art by the main-stream art community. In today's comic book profession, many artists hold degrees from respected art schools. Daniel Clowes, the artist who created the dark and suspenseful graphic novel *Ghost World*, is a graduate of the prestigious art college Pratt Institute in New York. Marjane Satrapi, who created the critically acclaimed graphic novel *Persepolis*, which tells of her childhood in Iran, attended the renowned École supérieure des arts décoratifs (National School of Decorative Arts) in Strasbourg, France.

Meanwhile, many museums have staged exhibitions of comic book art, among them the Oakland Museum in Oakland, California; the Musée d'Art Moderne in Paris; and the Whitney Museum and the Museum of Modern Art, both in New York City. Says Bill Kartalopoulos, a professor of illustration at the Parsons School of Design in New York City, "Comic books used to be considered pulp—disposable entertainment. That is no longer the case. Every bookstore has a graphic novel section and museums are doing shows about comics."[4] Adds Laura Hoptman, who curated a 2002 exhibition of comic book art at the Museum of Modern Art, "If you're going to talk about a traditional notion of what it means to draw—and draw well—you have to look at comics."[5]

> **Words in Context**
> *pulp*
> A term dating back to the early 1900s, when detective novels and similar thrillers, known as pulp fiction, were published on cheap paper and sold for pennies.

Comic books and the stories they tell have come a long way since their origins in the twentieth century. The artwork is more sophisticated and the stories more enticing. The stories and characters found on the pages of comic books have been adapted to other media, particularly film, TV, and video games. But the mission of the comic book remains the same as it was when the first issues rolled off the presses some seventy-five years ago: to deliver a highly entertaining and well-illustrated story to the many dedicated fans of the genre.

Chapter One

The Art of Telling Stories

Human thought is often sequential. In other words, humans can organize their thoughts in a straight line, linking them together in a logical progression. Asked by police to describe a bank robbery, an eyewitness is most likely to start at the instant when the robber walked into the bank and end with the moment the robber dashed out the door, making his or her getaway. Even planning a trip to the grocery store requires sequential thinking: The shopper prepares a shopping list before leaving for the store, rather than taking care of this chore while standing in the checkout line.

Although sequential thinking may seem easy, it is not. Humans are the only species on the planet known to think sequentially. Norman Cousins, the longtime editor of the magazine *Saturday Review*, suggested that no human endeavor is as difficult as putting one's thoughts in proper sequence. "It requires an almost limitless number of mental operations," he said. "The route must be anticipated between the present location of an idea and where it is supposed to go. Memory must be raked for relevant material. Facts or notions must be sorted out, put in their proper places, then supplied with connective tissue. Then comes the problem of weighting and emphasis."[6]

Art—which is a product of human thought—can be sequential as well. Sequential art is composed of a series of images laid out on a page or on the screen of a computer, tablet, or smartphone, requiring the viewer to observe each image in sequence in order to understand its meanings. A familiar form of sequential art is the comic strip published in the daily newspaper. In the typical newspaper comic, the cartoonist may require two, three, or four images to relate the message—usually a gag. Comic books are also a form of sequential art, but they are far more complicated than newspaper comics because comic books usually span dozens of pages. Moreover, graphic novels may span hundreds of pages.

Words and Illustrations

The composition of a comic book requires the writers and artists to devote tremendous amounts of sequential thinking to the tasks of plotting their stories, composing narration and dialogue, and envisioning how the events of the stories can be related in pictures. Says Roger Sabin, "Everything in a comic has to work—words, pictures, and timing—or else it fails. Sometimes, when it succeeds, it is capable of generating a thrill that is impossible in any other medium."[7]

Will Eisner, who wrote and illustrated comic books for more than sixty years before his death in 2005, suggested that in sequential art the writer and artist are doing the sequential thinking for the reader. "Sequential art is the act of weaving a fabric," he said. "In writing with words alone, the author directs the reader's imagination. In comics the imagining is done for the reader."[8]

Unlike most other forms of art, comic books contain literary elements: dialogue spoken by the characters as well as other bits of written narration dropped into the stories where they are necessary. Therefore, the composition of a comic book requires both words and illustrations. As such, writers and artists often collaborate on comic books. Typically, the writer provides a script to the artist, who then illustrates the story using the script as a guide. Many artists—among them Paul Pope, who has written and illustrated comic books featuring Batman, and Mike Mignola, who conceived the series featuring Hellboy—have established reputations as capable writers, meaning they provide both words and art to the finished books.

> **Words in Context**
> *sequential art*
> Art that tells a story, usually in the form of panels that feature both literary and illustrative elements.

How Comic Book Art Is Created

Comic book art is typically created in several stages. The process often involves multiple artists, each of whom specializes in a different stage of development.

An artist sketches images in pencil to match the story plot.

①

Often, another artist known as an inker uses pen and ink or a computer to sharpen the outlines.

②

③

Small details and larger areas are filled in.

Shading and color are added to create the finished comic.

④

In addition, although the script for a comic book may be produced by a single writer, it is not unusual for the illustrations to be rendered by teams of artists, particularly at large publishers like DC Comics and Marvel, which may publish fifty or more titles per month. Therefore, separate artists may be assigned to tasks on each title. Among these tasks are the initial pencil sketches of the main characters, the final inked versions of the action, the application of colors to the panels, the rendering of the lettering for the dialogue and narration, and the creation of the backgrounds in the panels.

Moving the Reader Through Time

Since all comic books include words and pictures, the composition of a comic book requires the combination of four literary and artistic elements: narrative breakdown, composition, layout, and style. The narrative breakdown of a comic book is how the writer and artist have elected to divide the story into separate images, or panels. The narrative breakdown is what makes a comic book sequential art. The story begins with the first panel on the first page and ends with the final panel on the final page, dozens of pages later. In between, the writer and artist have broken the action into separate panels, each dependent on the panel that comes before it. The narrative breakdown moves the reader through time, providing a sequential order for the story. "Narrative breakdown is the device by which timing is achieved; by manipulating time, the cartoonist produces dramatic effects,"[9] says Robert C. Harvey, an artist and comic book historian.

> **Words in Context**
> *layout*
> The artistic element of a comic book that focuses on how the panels are arranged on the page.

The composition is the artist's responsibility. It is simply how the artist wishes to portray the action in each specific panel. A panel showing Captain America throwing a punch could be illustrated from Captain America's point of view, providing readers with a view of the blow as it lands in the face of the thug. Or the scene could be illustrated from the thug's point of view, as the character watches the

Working as a Marvel Artist

Top artists for comic book publishers are usually freelance workers—they are not employees of Marvel, DC Comics, or other publishers but are hired to illustrate specific titles. Typically, they work at home or in studio space they may lease.

Still, the publishers do hire artists to work in-house, providing the final details on comic book art after it has been submitted by the freelance artists. Kate Levin, a young graphic designer, held such a position at Marvel for two years starting in 2006 before moving on to designing advertisements and other published materials.

Levin says she was assigned various tasks, such as adding the Marvel logo and text to comic book covers and designing the letters-from-readers pages found in Marvel comic books. Levin also had to find and correct errors made in the freelancers' art. A typical example is slight differences in the shades of colors from panel to panel. She says:

> I've since gone on to work in publishing and advertising, but I can say that Marvel prepared me for everything that I've had to do since. And nothing has compared to the workload of multiple weekly press publications. I've always been aware of how lucky I was to get that job, and how much it has taught me along the way. But mostly, I've been proud to say that I worked with Spider-Man (and if I ever have kids, that's exactly what I'm going to tell them!)

Kate Levin, "It Happened to Me: I Worked at Marvel Comics," *xoJane*, January 28, 2013. www.xojane.com.

hero's fist arrive home. Harvey likens comic book composition to the work of the cinematographer on a movie set, who decides what angles to employ when filming a scene.

Setting the Tone

Moreover, in the composition stage, the artist sets the tone for the panel. By creating expressions on the characters' faces or through the use of shadows or bright colors, the artist can establish the mood in the panel, making it humorous, suspenseful, sad, or upbeat. According to Eisner, "Functioning as a stage, the panel controls the viewpoint of the reader; the panel's outline becomes the perimeter of the reader's vision and establishes the perspective from which the site of the action is viewed. This manipulation enables the artist to clarify activity, orient the reader and stimulate emotion."[10]

Layout covers how the artist decides to arrange the panels on the page. In the early days of comic book publishing, most artists were locked into a tight grid dictated by their publishers. For years most comic book pages featured three panels across the top, three across the middle, and three across the bottom. Starting in the 1980s, as more talented artists entered the comic book industry and the ability to print comics became more sophisticated, publishers gave artists more freedom, permitting them to decide on the size, location, and number of panels per page. In today's world of comic book art, it is not unusual to see a grid of nine panels of equal size on a page, but it is also not unusual to see all manner of variations. These variations may include a single page devoted to the action in one panel. Or some pages may feature one panel that is far larger than another, one panel inserted into another, three panels of varying size, and so on.

> **Words in Context**
> *colorist*
> The artist responsible for adding colors to the panels after they have been sketched and inked by other artists.

Joseph Witek, an English professor at Stetson University in Florida and longtime observer of comic book art and narration, insists that the storytelling ability of writers and artists took a step forward when publishers released them from the rigid nine-panel format. Witek cites the *Watchmen* superhero series published by DC in 1986—written by Alan Moore and illustrated by artist Dave Gibbons and colorist John Higgins—as among the first comic books to break away from the nine-panel grid. He says, "Though extremely economical of space, highly regular grids tend inevitably toward both visual

The *Watchmen* comic book series, which featured these and other superheroes, was one of the first to break away from the rigid nine-panel format. The storytelling ability of writers and artists grew immensely once that change took place.

monotony and flatness in narrative action, since each event is given a similar visual weight whatever its importance in the story, so that a panel of mechanical plot exposition looks much the same as the slam-bang climax of the adventure."[11]

Visual and Verbal

In addition to composition and layout, the artist also provides the style—the final creative element found in comic book art. Style reflects the signature method of the artist. Every person who has ever dabbled in art, regardless of the medium, has brought his or her individual style to the work. Descriptions of the work of two noted illustrators reveal how style can vary widely from artist to artist in comic books. Describing the work of Mignola, creator of Hellboy (a hulky demon summoned from the Underworld to fight for justice), the entertainment news website A.V. Club explains: "As he let his imagination run rampant, his artwork grew darker, more experimental, and more daring: abstract backgrounds, rough faces, exaggerated anatomy, and impenetrable pools of shadow became his hallmarks."[12] Dan DeCarlo, who created the series *Josie and the Pussycats* (featuring members of a mystery-solving girl rock band) as well as *Sabrina the Teenage Witch*, offered a stark contrast to the work of Mignola. The A.V. Club assessed DeCarlo's lighthearted style: "Much of [his] appeal remains rooted in DeCarlo's simple, clean lines and appealing, easy-to-recognize characters."[13]

Comic book writers and artists employ these four elements—narrative breakdown, composition, layout, and style—to merge the visual side of comic books with the verbal side. According to Harvey, wedding the visual with the verbal is the chief challenge in producing a comic book. The words and pictures must be used in tandem, each complementing the other. If the villain is cackling a threat, the words uttered by the bad guy must fit the scenario. Likewise, the composition and mood of the panel must fit the scenario as well.

Words and Pictures in Sync

Perhaps no figure in the comic book industry understands the importance of merging the visual with the verbal better than Stan Lee, who started writing scripts for comic books in the 1940s and went on to become publisher of Marvel. For a comic book to work, he says, words and pictures must be in perfect sync:

I think that the art has always been at least as important as the story. Because you can tell the best story in the world, but if the artwork is dull—it's like a movie: If the photography, acting, or directing is bad, you can have a great story but it's still not going to be a great movie. By the same token, you can have

Zap, Pow, and Oof

One method of merging words with pictures is the way in which comic book artists and writers use their talents to portray action. Merely showing Captain America throwing a punch at a bad guy does not completely do the job of displaying the excitement of the moment. Therefore, artists and writers frequently add what are known as onomatopoeic (pronounced *ono-mato-pee-ic*) words: They use language to imitate sounds. Any comic book reader is familiar with these words. Drawn large and lively, they are sprinkled throughout the panels wherever they are needed: *boom, bang, crack, clunk, ping, zap, pow,* and *oof,* among others.

The word *onomatopoeia* finds its roots in the ancient Greek language. *Onoma* means "name" and *poeia* means "making." Explains Ursula Dubosarsky, an Australian writer of young people's literature, "Onomatopoeia is when you use a name or word that makes the sound of something, or at least suggests it somehow. For an easy example, remember the fights in Batman? *POW! WHAM! SMASH!* That's onomatopoeia. Comic book writers love it."

She adds that people often substitute words for sounds in everyday speech. Anybody who imitates the sound of a duck by using the word *quack* or the sound of a cow by uttering the word *moo* has used onomatopoeia.

Ursula Dubosarsky, *The Word Snoop*. New York: Penguin, 2009. Kindle edition.

the best artwork and if the story isn't there, you're only going to appeal to people who like to look at nice drawings. To me, a comic [book] should be a beautifully illustrated story, not just beautiful illustrations. . . .

We always tried to have dialogue that sounded as if real people might say it, and we always tried to give our characters different personalities so they weren't cut from the same mold. We tried to have each one talking differently from the others. But, getting back to the original statement, we never concentrated more on script than art, nor did we concentrate more on art than script. The two are indivisible: they had to work perfectly together.[14]

Floating Balloons

As Lee suggests, in a comic book the words and art are of equal importance. So a major challenge facing the writer and artist who collaborate on a comic book is to know when to use dialogue and narration to tell the story and when to use just illustration to move the story along. According to Eisner, there is no rule that dictates how many words can be used in a comic book. Therefore, the writer and artist must work very closely together to decide when the illustrative elements of a panel should do more to tell the story than the text that is employed in the panel or when spoken dialogue is essential to the story. "There is absolutely no ratio of words-to-picture in a medium where words (lettering) are in themselves part of the form,"[15] he said.

In the comic book, dialogue is related in a balloon—words encased in a graphic element that floats near the character in the panel. During the early years of comic book art, the balloons were usually round or oval and were drawn with a point that emanated from the character's mouth—leaving no doubt as to who was saying what. In more contemporary times, some artists have been able to add dialogue to a panel by floating the words in space near the characters.

Words in Context

balloon

An artistic component of a comic book, often drawn as a circle or oval, containing the text spoken by characters.

Comic book stories usually result from collaboration between an artist and writer. The two work together to decide where and when to use illustration and where and when to use dialogue to tell the story.

How they elect to add text to their panels does not really matter, as long as the reader clearly understands which character is uttering the words. The layout of dialogue in a panel must be sequential, meaning a back and forth conversation between characters has to be easy to follow by the readers. "A major requirement is that they be read in a prescribed sequence in order to know who speaks first,"[16] said Eisner.

In addition, artists are able to add emphasis to the speech of the character through various graphic techniques. A character's words that are thought but not spoken, for example, may be represented in a balloon resembling a cloud. Words that are spoken over a television or radio are often rendered in a balloon that features a jagged outline—giving the text an electric feel.

Balloons can also be employed to help the artist illustrate emotions and other human reactions in their characters. To illustrate words that are shouted, the artist may use larger text characters or make them darker and bolder (the technical term is *boldface*) to make them stand out. If a character is whispering, the balloon may be drawn with a dashed outline and small lettering to illustrate how the words are spoken softly. An icicle balloon is illustrated with icicles dripping from the lower edge, illustrating how the character's emotion is cold toward someone or something. A balloon shaded in red may illustrate anger, and a balloon shaded green may indicate envy. To illustrate a character's singing voice, the artist may draw musical notes around the balloon or intermingle the notes with the spoken text. To show how an idea may occur to a character, the artist may draw a lightbulb over the character's head. The balloon for a sleeping character may be filled with the letter *Z*. To illustrate shock or surprise, the artist may draw lines shooting out from the character's head. Profanities uttered by a character are illustrated in the balloon by using typographical characters, such as *?*$@!* Wiggly lines around a character's head may indicate nervousness. Drips of water flying off a character's head may indicate worry. Little stars and half-moons drawn around a character's head are used to indicate dizziness.

Concept of the Comic Book

Although artists and writers have long relied on these techniques to provide drama to their stories, the art of composing comic books has changed over the decades. Artists are no longer confined to the rigid nine-panel format long dictated by publishers. Balloons have taken on new shapes—or no shape at all. And artists whose styles are as varied as Mignola's and DeCarlo's have lent their talents to the medium. Nevertheless, throughout the history of the comic book the basic concept has never changed. Comic books are the most familiar example of sequential art—a medium that closely reflects the way people commonly string their thoughts together.

Chapter Two

Conquest of the Superheroes

The first superhero whose adventures were featured on the pages of a comic book was Superman, who made his debut in June 1938. Since then, Superman has grown into a true cultural icon, appearing in thousands of other comic book adventures as well as stories depicted in other media: TV, radio, movies, video games, and even the Broadway stage. But it was another superhero, Captain America, who is perhaps most responsible for making comic books into the primary source of literature in which readers find stories about these larger-than-life mythical figures.

Conceived by artists Joe Simon and Jack Kirby, Captain America made his debut on the newsstands in an issue dated March 1941. By then World War II had already erupted in Europe, but America was not yet involved in the conflict. Still, many Americans feared the inevitable: that the war would spread and the United States would eventually be drawn into the fight against Nazi Germany. In East Coast cities such as New York and Boston, residents worried about enemy bombers attacking from above or German submarines infiltrating their ports. Clearly, a hero was needed to ease troubled minds.

And so while Superman thwarted the evil intentions of assorted crooks, Captain America's adventures were aimed more toward national security. Wearing a red, white, and blue costume resembling the Stars and Stripes, Captain America battled spies, saboteurs, and others who threatened the American way of life.

In fact, the cover of his premiere adventure depicts Captain America throwing a punch across the chin of Nazi dictator Adolf Hitler. Simon recalls how he first envisioned Captain America:

The comics that were doing really well at the time were ones with clever villains in them, so I started by looking around for the perfect villain. I tossed out a lot of ideas, but then I realized that we had the perfect guy right in front of us. I thought to myself, *let's get a real villain.* Adolf Hitler would be the perfect foil for our next character, what with his hair and that stupid-looking mustache and his goose-stepping. He was like a cartoon anyway.

Now we needed a hero who would go up against Hitler. Even though the United States wasn't at war, we read the newspapers. We knew what was happening in Europe, and we were outraged by the Nazis—totally outraged. We thought it was a good time for a patriotic hero.[17]

Ideal Medium for Superheroics

Simon and Kirby emphasized Captain America's physique, depicting the hero as tall and muscular. His demeanor was serious and his mission clear: to protect America against all enemies, foreign and domestic—but mostly foreign. Says Roger Sabin, "Captain America, by Joe Simon and Jack Kirby, was the embodiment of American patriotism during the Second World War."[18] In fact, the first comic book featuring the adventures of Captain America sold nearly 1 million copies, smashing all comic book sales records to date.

That was a message absorbed by the still very young comic book industry of the 1940s, and soon publishers assigned writers and artists to concoct characters and adventures copying those of Captain America. Within months, heroes such as American Avenger, American Crusader, Commando Yank, Fighting Yank, Yankee Boy, Yankee Doodle

The cover of Captain America's first comic book adventure features the star-spangled hero punching Nazi leader Adolf Hitler. Captain America's creators wanted to depict a patriotic hero who would battle spies, saboteurs, and anyone else who threatened the American way of life.

Jones, Flagman, Captain Flag, Captain Glory, and Captain Victory made their debuts on the pages of comic books. None of those copycat heroes had the staying power of Captain America, who still appears in adventures today. All those characters eventually disappeared by war's end, largely because their creators lacked the talents of Kirby and Simon.

Still, Captain America's success, along with the efforts by other publishers to copy his adventures, helped establish comic books as the primary place readers could find stories about heroes with special powers. Says Robert C. Harvey:

> Superheroes and comic books were made for each other. In symbiotic reciprocity, they contributed to each other's success. Superheroes in comics sparked a demand for comics— and that demand created the need for original superhero material, written and drawn expressly for the medium. Comic books were the ideal medium for portraying the exploits of super beings. They were nearly the only medium at the time. You could write about superheroes in novels, or you could film their adventures. But neither books nor movies were quite up to the task of depicting superheroes' impossible feats. Books lacked the conviction, the authority and impact, of visuals. And in the movies, the incredible deeds of superheroes looked phony: the film technology of the day had not yet developed the sophisticated special effects necessary to give the celluloid images an authentic feel. But comic books made superheroics both palpable and probable.[19]

From Krypton to Kansas

Captain America's vigilance against foreign enemies may have endeared him to American readers, but Superman was nevertheless the first comic book character to establish the medium as the home of the superhero. By now even casual fans are familiar with the story of Superman. He was born on the planet Krypton, which at the time faced destruction. To save their baby, whom they named Kal-El, his parents put him aboard a rocket ship and launched him on a journey to Earth. The ship crashed-landed on the Kansas farm of Ma and Pa Kent, who discovered the baby

Manga: Comic Books in Japan

Peach Girl, a popular comic book series in Japan, follows character Momo Adachi as she makes her way through high school, enduring the jealousies of backstabbing rivals while swooning over the latest heartthrobs who come in and out of her life. Momo is known as Peach Girl because of her strawberry blonde hair.

Peach Girl is an example of manga—a word that translates into English as "random pictures." Although comic books may enjoy wide popularity in the United States as well as in many other countries, in Japan they have a truly enormous appeal among readers. For example, the most widely read periodical in America is the newsmagazine *Time*, which has a weekly circulation of about 3 million. That is roughly the circulation of *Weekly Shōnen Jump*—one of Japan's most popular manga publications.

Manga is published for readers of all ages. Young boys read *shōnen*, the Japanese word for "boy." *Shōnen* titles usually focus on adventure stories. Likewise, young girls read *shojo*, the Japanese word for "girl." *Shojo* stories focus on young female characters and their relationships—*Peach Girl* is a *shojo* series. Teenage girls read *shōnen ai* (boy love), which introduce romance into the stories. *Seinen* (young man) manga is written and illustrated for adult male readers. *Seinen* stories usually focus on adventures, but readers can expect to find a strong dose of violence and sexual content. A very popular *seinen* series follows the adventures of a Japanese swordsman known as Vagabond.

and raised him as their own, naming him Clark. As a teenager, Clark discovered his superpowers. He went on to work as a reporter for the *Daily Planet* and always be ready to save humankind. In real life, Superman's roots are far more mundane: He was actually born in Cleveland, Ohio—a creation of teenagers Jerry Siegel and Joe Shuster.

The story of how Siegel and Shuster created Superman begins in 1933. At the time, the adventures of detective Dick Tracy had started appearing on the comics pages of daily newspapers. To capitalize on Tracy's popularity, Chicago artist Norman Marsh produced a cheap knockoff of the no-nonsense cop. He named his character Detective Dan. Unlike Tracy, though, Detective Dan's story was not told in the format of a comic strip but as a slim paperback magazine. Fans of Dick Tracy had to follow the story in the newspapers over the course of weeks or months to see how the hard-nosed cop solved crimes. On the other hand, readers of *Detective Dan* could read the whole story, start to finish, in one sitting.

Marsh and his publisher, Consolidated Publishing, have cemented their place in the history of publishing by producing what is regarded as the first comic book. There had been magazine-sized comic books published before *Detective Dan* hit the newsstands. However, these were simply reprints of comic strips that had already been published in the daily and Sunday newspapers. *Detective Dan* was the first original comic book that told of the adventures of a character with a story that was new to readers.

Pulp Fiction Fans

Siegel discovered a copy of *Detective Dan* on a newsstand in his hometown of Cleveland. He bought a copy and read through it quickly, then showed it to his best friend, Shuster, a talented artist. (The two met while working on their high school newspaper; Siegel as a writer and Shuster as a cartoonist.) Siegel and Shuster were both devoted readers of pulp fiction magazines such as *Amazing Stories*, *Astounding Stories*, and *Weird Tales*. However, the pulps featured few illustrations—mostly just lurid covers invariably displaying shapely damsels in peril.

Siegel and Shuster were a pair of underachievers. Neither studied too hard—both young men preferred reading the pulps to their social studies and math books—and both had to spend an extra year in high school to graduate. Between them, though, they had been working out an idea for a comic strip they hoped to sell to newspapers, with Siegel providing the story and Shuster the art.

Superman cocreator Joe Shuster drew this 1938 caricature of his partner Jerry Siegel (left) and himself (right) being hefted above the city by their comic book creation: Superman. Shuster, an artist, and Siegel, a writer, developed their idea while still in high school.

The character they concocted was a crime fighter, but not in the style of Dick Tracy or Detective Dan. Their character—whom they named Superman—was gifted with superhuman powers: He possessed the ability to fly and could also count on super strength, X-ray vision, heat vision, and invulnerability, among other abilities. "Our concept would be to combine the best traits of all the heroes of history,"[20] explained Shuster.

They pitched their idea to a number of syndicates—services that sell comic strips and other features to newspapers—always receiving polite rejections. But then Siegel saw a copy of *Detective Dan* and realized this new comic book format was an ideal medium to tell the story of their hero. They wrote to Consolidated Publishing and received a letter expressing interest. "We have delayed in responding until we could give the matter of 'The Superman' deliberate consideration," wrote the publisher. "Should we desire to put out another edition of *Detective Dan*, if the author and the artist is not agreeable, we will then be glad to take up the matter with you, with a view of publishing 'The Superman' instead of *Detective Dan*."[21] When they received the letter of interest from Consolidated, Siegel and Shuster had just graduated from high school. Siegel worked at a printing plant, earning four dollars a week; Shuster worked as a delivery boy for a grocery store, also earning a meager wage.

New Crime Fighters

As things turned out, Marsh decided against producing a follow-up edition of *Detective Dan*. Instead, the character was picked up by a comic strip syndicate and sold to newspapers, which published the detective's adventures under a comic strip called *Dan Dunn*. With Marsh dropping out, the way seemed clear for the first edition of *Superman*—but it was not to be. Due to the dismal sales of *Detective Dan*, Consolidated Publishing elected to get out of the comic book business.

Siegel and Shuster were devastated. It took another five years for the two friends to find a publisher. By 1938 other publishers had started printing comic books, finding a bit more success than Consolidated. In the meantime, some fantastic characters had started showing up in the newspaper comic strips. Among them were Tarzan, the jungle lord whose adventures were based on the novels by Edgar Rice Burroughs; Flash Gordon, an interstellar traveler and adventurer; and a character named the Phantom, a crime fighter

> **Words in Context**
> *syndicate*
> An organization that markets written and artistic features, such as comic strips and columns by political commentators, to newspapers and magazines.

who wore a mask and purple tights. None of these characters possessed superpowers, but the idea that a character other than a policeman like Dick Tracy could fight the bad guys had gained traction with the public.

Finally, some sample comic strips featuring Superman came to the attention of Vin Sullivan, a New York publishing executive. Sullivan contacted Siegel and Shuster and asked them to produce a comic book version of Superman. Siegel and Shuster eagerly complied, and in June 1938 the first issue of *Action Comics* hit the newsstands. The cover depicted the hero, clad in a blue-and-red costume, showing off his super strength by hoisting an automobile over his head.

Despite its place as trendsetter for all superhero comics to come, issue number one of *Action Comics* was something less than high artistic achievement. "The art is still immature, the faces unvaryingly passive: two quick horizontal slits for eyes, one for the nose,"[22] says *New Yorker* magazine writer Deborah Friedell. Moreover, Siegel's early scripts hardly portrayed Superman as a role model for the young people who were expected to be the primary readers of *Action Comics*. Instead of respecting the rights of the accused, Superman was more likely to toss the crooks out of skyscraper windows.

Superheroes with Human Emotions

Action Comics featuring Superman was published by the New York company Detective Comics, eventually to be known as DC Comics. A year after Superman made his debut, the publisher introduced Batman. Over the next several years, additional superhero characters—Aquaman, Wonder Woman, the Flash, and Green Lantern, among others—were introduced.

By the early 1960s DC was facing serious competition from Marvel, which added a different kind of superhero to the genre. Stan Lee, the Marvel executive who created most of the company's characters, wanted the Marvel superheroes to have superpowers, but he also wanted them to have very human qualities as well.

The first superheroes created under Lee were members of the Fantastic Four—a quartet of heroes that included the leader, Reed Richards, who can stretch his body like rubber; Johnny Storm, the

The Popularity of Underground Comics

During the 1960s and 1970s, so-called underground comics exploded in popularity. Often crudely drawn, the comic books were read mostly by college students and other young people who embraced the counterculture—the culture of "hippie" life, drug use, promiscuous sex, and opposition to the Vietnam War. During this era, the most popular of the underground comics was *Zap Comix*, first published in 1968. Says Roger Sabin, a professor at Central Saint Martin's College of Art and Design in London, "Unlike conventional comics, underground strips were not created in a production-line environment. Writers and artists, inkers and letterers were not teamed up to work under the control of one editor. Instead, the underground creator controlled every facet of his or her creation."

The adventures of superheroes were not portrayed in the pages of *Zap* and the other underground publications. Rather, the typical characters were pot-smoking slackers, outlaw bikers, rock musicians, and assorted petty thieves and con artists.

The leading artist for *Zap* was Robert Crumb, and his most memorable character was Fritz the Cat. Fritz was a cat who walked and talked like a human, wore clothes, and was supposedly a student at New York University—although he never seemed to attend classes. Instead, Fritz was far more interested in the party life as well as other hedonistic pursuits. By the late 1970s, though, the underground comics movement had all but died off, largely because most readers of *Zap* and the other titles had outgrown the counterculture.

Roger Sabin, *Comics, Comix & Graphic Novels: A History of Comic Art*. London: Phaidon, 2014, p. 94.

human torch; his sister, Sue Storm, who possesses the power of invisibility; and Ben Grimm, also known as the Thing, who is gifted with super strength but is plagued by skin composed of rocks. According to Lee's biographers, Jordan Raphael and Tom Spurgeon, "The Fantastic Four weren't as invincible as Superman or as crafty as Batman. They didn't even wear costumes until their third outing. Sure, they had super powers, but they were defined as much by their weaknesses as their strengths. The FF teammates felt resentment, got depressed, and bickered among themselves like family. In short, they were human. Or they were at least closer to possessing human qualities than any of their spandex-clad predecessors."[23]

In addition to the Fantastic Four, other superheroes added to the Marvel stable have included Thor, Iron Man, Incredible Hulk, Spider-Man, Daredevil, and others. And DC has expanded its stable of superheroes as well. The publisher produces stories featuring dozens of superheroes, ranging from Atom—in real life, physicist Ray Palmer, who can shrink himself down to subatomic size, using the power to battle evil—to Zatanna Zatara, a magician who has discovered her fantastical gifts by reciting spells backward.

Classics Illustrated

Although Superman, Batman, Spider-Man, and other superheroes dominate the pages of comic books, over the years publishers have produced stories depicting characters who cannot fly or punch their way through brick walls and have no interest at all in nabbing crooks, spies, or evil scientists. Before folding in 1977, the comic book series *Young Romance*, produced solely for a female audience, featured boy-meets-girl love stories, none of which included spandex-wearing superheroes. In 1941 Albert Kanter, who was working as a publisher's sales representative—he pitched titles to bookstore owners—established *Classic Comics*. The publisher specialized in retelling classic works of fiction in a comic book format. Over the course of thirty years, *Classic Comics*—later known as *Classics Illustrated*—published comic book versions of books such as Charles Dickens's *Oliver Twist*, Mark Twain's *A Connecticut Yankee in King Arthur's Court*, Robert Louis Stevenson's *Dr. Jekyll and Mr. Hyde*, and Jonathan Swift's *Gulliver's Travels*.

Like all comic book heroes, Marvel's characters had remarkable powers. But under Stan Lee (pictured in the early 2000s) the superheroes appearing in Marvel comic books also demonstrated a variety of human frailties.

Novelist Anne Rice, whose books include the horror classic *Interview with the Vampire*, recalled poring through *Classics Illustrated* comic books as a young girl. Among her favorites were comic book versions of *Jane Eyre* by Charlotte Brontë and *Moby-Dick* by Herman Melville. "Not only did these comics give us an appreciation for novels we would later read, they were a thrilling art form in themselves," she says. "I can still remember some of the drawings quite vividly."[24]

Amazing Stories

Meanwhile, in 1941, as famous characters from literature found their way onto the pages of comic books, girl-crazy teenager Archie Andrews and his friends—Betty, Veronica, and Jughead—made their debuts as well. Their antics continue to be illustrated today by a publishing company that has adopted the name of its most famous character: Archie Comics. And although the typical Archie adventure may find Archie and Veronica in a spat over where to lay down their beach blanket, even the executives at Archie Comics know the value of a good superhero story. A subsidiary of Archie Comics, Dark Circle Comics, publishes numerous superhero series, featuring characters such as Black Hood, the Fox, the Shield, and the Hangman—all of whom are mysterious heroes who fight evil.

The fact that Archie Comics sees the need to publish stories about superheroes illustrates how these mythical figures have come to dominate the art of the comic book. Since the days when Superman threw evildoers out of skyscraper windows and Captain America punched Hitler off his feet, publishers have known readers find the comic book the ideal medium for telling these amazing stories.

Chapter Three

Comic Books Enter the Dark Side

Starting in the late 1960s, comic book sellers began noticing a change in their customers. Until then, the typical comic book buyer was male and either a preteen or teenager. By 1967, when the first US store devoted exclusively to comic book sales opened in San Francisco, the age of the fan base seemed to be changing. Young men in their twenties—hooked on the adventures of Batman, Green Lantern, the Flash, and Spider-Man since their preteen years—began frequenting stores like the San Francisco Comic Book Company. This new demographic was not lost on comic book publishers, who began urging their writers to approach their stories and characters in a different way. Publishers knew they were now producing comic books for a slightly older audience. This meant that the traditional theme of the comic book—one in which the good superhero battles, and invariably defeats, an evil nemesis—had to change.

No Longer Good Versus Evil

Marvel was the first publisher to recognize the need to change the old good-versus-evil formula. In 1975 it added new characters to the X-Men, one of whom was Wolverine. To be sure, the character was a superhero—he possessed werewolf-like powers—but Wolverine was hardly cut from the same cloth as Captain America. Indeed, whenever Wolverine slashed an evildoer to death with the huge metal talons that emerged from his knuckles, he seemed to enjoy it. By the early 1980s *The Uncanny X-Men* emerged as the most popular series in the comic book genre.

DC responded by resuscitating *Swamp Thing*, which it had ceased publishing in 1976. A human turned into a slimy green monster at home in the swamps, Swamp Thing was like any other superhero—a good guy who battled evil. In 1982 DC called on writer Alan Moore and artists Stephen Bissette and John Totleben to reinvent Swamp Thing for an older audience. Moore and the artists introduced politically relevant topics into the plots of Swamp Thing adventures, among them feminism, drug abuse, gun laws, and environmentalism. Says Maggie Gray, an art historian at University College London:

> The trailblazing team of Moore, Stephen Bissette and John Totleben reconceived the title radically as a genre-blurring mash-up of psychological terror, gothic romance, and science fiction adventure. The central character is transformed from a tragic hybrid into a plant god intrinsically connected to all vegetable life, using its powers to become as large as a mountain or as small as flora in the human body. This gives a powerful agency to the natural world. . . . Swamp Thing is also important because of the radical way it advocates environmentalism. The series explores issues such as pollution, deforestation, and the threat of toxic waste.[25]

Offset Printing Arrives

By now the stories had grown up, but the artwork of the comic book seemed no different than it had for years. The nine-panel format still prevailed. Artists tended to use bright colors. And overwhelmingly, comic book artists belonged to the realism school of art, meaning their images resembled photographic representations of real life.

Meanwhile, a dramatic improvement in the quality of the actual printing of comic books occurred in the 1970s. Back

By the 1970s most publishers of comic books and other media had switched to offset printing presses (pictured). Offset printing made possible higher-quality reproduction which, in turn, led to more-sophisticated comic book illustrations.

when *Action Comics* was first published in 1938, comic books—along with newspapers, magazines, and other publications—were printed in what is known as the letterpress process. Letterpress is actually the style of printing first pioneered by Johannes Gutenberg in the 1400s when he invented the printing press. In letterpress, text and images are cast in metal, with the inked surfaces raised higher than the portions of the page that will be white. (The white areas of the paper are not inked.) Each of four basic colors—magenta (red), cyan (blue), yellow, and black—are then applied separately to the image, meaning the paper has to run through the press four times. Letterpress works better in black and white than in color, because if one or more colors are applied the slightest bit off the mark (in the printing trade, it is known as out of register), the images show up on the pages with minor, yet evident, blurs.

During the 1970s most publishers—including the publishers of comic books—had switched to offset printing. In offset printing, the colors are still applied separately, but the images are inked onto rubber sheets, which come into contact with the paper. In offset printing, the application of the ink tends to be more accurate. And since offset printing provides higher-quality reproductions, the process is able to reproduce more sophisticated illustrations.

Expressionism in Comic Book Art

This more sophisticated printing process found an ideal showcase in 1979 when Marvel assigned artist Frank Miller to a title in the *Daredevil* series. Marvel published the first comic book featuring Daredevil in 1964, telling the story of Matt Murdock, a young man who loses his vision in an accident. Finding his other senses have grown so acute that he is able to navigate through life without vision, Murdock assumes a secret identity—Daredevil—to fight crime. In his first case, Daredevil avenges the death of his father, a prizefighter who was killed by gangsters after refusing to throw a fight.

In taking over *Daredevil*, Miller helped revolutionize comic book art. He broke away from the school of realism and instead drew inspiration from the artistic movement known as expressionism. The movement traces its roots to Germany during the first three decades of the twentieth century—a dim era for the German people. After suffering defeat in World War I, they found their country beset by urban blight, poverty, hunger, anger, and divisive politics. This attitude was reflected in the work of the artists of the era, who displayed their emotions in their paintings. In other words, the expressionist does not depict a scene on canvas as the camera may have photographed it, but from the way in which the scene touches the emotions of the artist. In an expressionist painting, images of people or buildings may be distorted, colors may be wildly inappropriate, and points of view turned upside down.

Words in Context
expressionism
An artistic style in which the emotions of the artist are reflected in a scene, which tends to alter the image from a realistic or camera-like view.

Girls, Women, and Comic Books

When the first comic book stores started opening in the 1960s, the owners noticed their customers were not limited to teens and preteens—many young adults were sifting through the racks. They also noticed that they had few female customers.

Comic book publishers have made many attempts over the years to lure female readers by introducing superheroines into their pages—DC introduced Wonder Woman in 1941, and invisible girl Sue Storm, a member of the Fantastic Four, was introduced by Marvel in 1961. Batgirl and Supergirl soon followed. In contemporary times the ranks of the superheroines include characters such as Black Canary, Raven, Natasha Irons, Elektra, and Mystique.

Even so, girls and young women are known to make up a small fraction of comic book readership. Critics suggest that comic books frequently portray women as victims or villains, and when they are portrayed as heroes they are invariably pictured as trim, athletic, and sexy—images that are more appealing to male readers than female readers. "They consistently make editorial decisions that seem designed to alienate women," says comic book artist Jessica Abel, who has also taught cartooning courses at the School of Visual Arts in New York. "So it's self-reinforcing. If you're constantly straight-arming women, women aren't going to read them. If they don't read them, they don't grow up imagining them. If they don't grow up imagining them, they're not going to [write and draw] them."

Quoted in Noelene Clark, "Women in Comics and the Tricky Art of Equality," *Los Angeles Times*, July 21, 2012. http://herocomplex.latimes.com.

Expressionism has found its way into other art forms as well. In the 1940s and 1950s, a movement in Hollywood films known as film noir—a French term that means "black film"—dominated the movie industry. Film noir features dark, somber stories, mostly filmed at night, and mostly featuring plots that involve murder and other crimes. In film noir the heroes are not always the good guys.

Darker and More Dangerous

This was the style Miller hoped to reflect in *Daredevil*. Moreover, Miller soon took over writing the scripts for the series as well, which enabled him to make the stories as dark as the artwork. Says Graphic NYC, a website that reports on trends in the comic book industry:

> Daredevil's New York, under Frank's run, became darker and more dangerous. . . . New York City itself, particularly Daredevil's Hell's Kitchen neighborhood, became as much a character as the shadowy crime fighter; the stories often took place on the rooftop level, with water towers, pipes and chimneys

Frank Miller's *Daredevil* series had the dark, edgy quality of the artistic movement known as expressionism. Expressionism also found a voice in the film noir style of moviemaking (pictured) which became popular in the 1940s and 1950s.

jutting out to create a skyline reminiscent of German Expressionism's dramatic edges and shadows. . . .

By the time Miller wrapped up his first run on *Daredevil* [in 1983], the character had gone from a predictable superhero archetype to a tortured (and very human) hero struggling to stay on the side of the angels. Matt Murdock wasn't just a son who avenged his murdered father by dressing up in tights: he was now the son of a washed-up alcoholic boxer of a Dad, who grows up teetering on the razor's edge between good and evil . . . always threatening to tip over to the wrong side. What Miller created in Daredevil wasn't necessarily an anti-hero, but a hero who was never too far from becoming a villain.[26]

Reinventing Batman

Daredevil was an instant success. Soon after Miller took over the art and writing, it became Marvel's second-best-selling series, just behind *The Uncanny X-Men*. DC responded to the trend first by luring Miller away from Marvel and asking him to develop a new and expressionist view of Batman. By the 1980s Batman as well as Superman were the publisher's most recognizable characters. By the time Miller took over Batman, though, the character had been through some bumpy times. In the late 1960s, the ABC television network produced a weekly series, *Batman*, which never took itself too seriously. The campy version featured cartoonish action, thin plots, wooden acting, and villains too funny to be feared—among them the Joker, Penguin, and Riddler. So the young people who watched Batman portrayed on TV in the late 1960s harbored that vision of the Caped Crusader as they reached adulthood in the 1970s and 1980s.

Miller aimed to change the world's view of Batman with the comic book series *Batman: The Dark Knight Returns*. When the initial issue was published in February 1986, it hardly resembled the campy version of Batman that TV viewers remembered from the

1960s. Miller's Batman had entered middle age—within the first few pages readers learn Batman is now fifty-five years old. Since retiring from crime fighting ten years earlier, Batman's home of Gotham City had turned into a city reminiscent of the German city of Berlin in the 1920s—impoverished, decadent, and under the thumb of gangsters. Says Roger Sabin:

> *Batman: The Dark Knight Returns* was a radical reconceptualization of bat-mythology, and distanced the character as far from his campy 1960s incarnation as it was possible to go. In this version, a cynical and twisted Batman, driven by inner demons, comes out of retirement to wage his last fateful campaign against the Joker. In the resulting carnage, his vigilante motivations are exposed—and celebrated. For Miller, the new Batman was "a moral force, a judge, plainly bigger and greater than normal men, and perfectly willing to pass judgment and administer punishment and make things right". . . .
>
> Artistically speaking, *Dark Knight* marked a progression from Miller's already slick Daredevil style: his use of shadow turned Gotham City into a noirish nightmare. . . . The result was a uniquely atmospheric, and menacing, comic.[27]

Scowling and Angry Superheroes

Dark Knight lasted a mere four issues in 1986, but other artists soon adopted Miller's style. DC's *Watchmen* series was very much in the same vein as Miller's *Batman*. Written by Moore and illustrated by Dave Gibbons and John Higgins, the *Watchmen* series was launched in 1986. Published as the United States and the former Soviet Union escalated their long-standing nuclear arms race, *Watchmen* reflected the growing horror among many people that the world was teetering on the edge of annihilation. Sharing in this angst were the *Watchmen* superheroes, whose struggles with their own inner demons were depicted by the artist's dark and expressionistic illustrations.

As comic books entered the twenty-first century, other artists have brought expressionist visions to the artwork as well as the stories told in comic books. Among them is Jim Lee, who joined the Marvel

Frank Miller

After growing up in Montpelier, Vermont, Frank Miller left for New York City in 1976 at age nineteen. A lifelong comic book fan, Miller spent his youth making his own sketches of comic characters. Self-taught as an artist, Miller carried his portfolio of sketches from publisher to publisher, meeting constant rejection. Throughout this period, Miller lived in small rented rooms and existed mostly on peanut butter sandwiches. Finally, Miller met Neal Adams, who provided the artwork for several titles for *Batman*. Adams saw talent in Miller's work and helped him refine his style. In 1979 Miller landed an assignment to provide the artwork for *Daredevil*.

Miller's dark visions of Daredevil's world helped establish expressionism as the predominant style in comic book art. His work on *Batman: The Dark Knight Returns* solidified that style. The incident that inspired Miller to portray Batman as angry and embittered, and Gotham City as a dark and dismal center of urban decay, occurred shortly before he took on the project. Since moving to New York, Miller had been robbed three times. He had just been paid for a job and still had the check in his pocket when a thief tried to steal it. "Frank just went berserk on the guy," says Lynn Varley, a colorist who later married Miller. "He didn't hit him or anything, he just went so berserk the guy backed off and ran away."

Quoted in Sean Howe, "After His Public Downfall, Sin City's Frank Miller Is Back (and Not Sorry)," *Wired*, August 20, 2014. www.wired.com.

artistic team in 1989 and was soon assigned to *The Uncanny X-Men*. After several years of work at Marvel, and after attempting to launch his own comic book publishing company, Lee joined DC, where he has illustrated titles for *Superman* and *Batman*. In illustrating the two superheroes, Lee relies heavily on shadows. The characters wear somber expressions of toughness. Adventures are usually staged at night, displaying dark edges to Superman's home city of Metropolis and Batman's home in Gotham City. And when the action takes place in daylight, the skies are invariably cloudy. "Lee's style has taken on a somewhat more visceral and expressionist quality,"[28] says Marc-Oliver Frisch, who contributes columns on the comic book industry to the trade journal *Publishers Weekly* and other publications. In 2010 Lee's style had become so pervasive at DC that he was named copublisher of the organization.

Another character that has been reinvented is Marvel's Incredible Hulk. Artist Leinil Francis Yu has changed the character's name to the Indestructible Hulk, making the green giant even angrier, more muscle-bound, and more inwardly troubled than his earlier incarnations. Yu prefers a style that makes the characters appear as though they are constantly emerging from dense smoke—giving his scenes a dreamy but haunted look. Wolverine has also been made even darker by Yu; his version of the longtime Marvel character shows a scowling, angry superhero.

Superman the Socialist

As the art has grown darker in recent years the stories have as well. Scottish writer Mark Millar has worked for both DC and Marvel as well as for smaller publishers. He has taken some of the most familiar names in comic books into strange territory. In 2003 Millar authored *Superman: Red Son*, in which Superman as a baby lands not in Kansas but in the former Soviet Union. The story envisions the superhero growing up in the Soviet totalitarian society. Rather than working as a defender of freedom and justice, Superman has bought into the fiction of the socialist state—where all property in a society is owned and shared equally by the people. In Millar's version, Superman dedicates his life to guarding the lowly Soviet citizens against the tyranny of Western capitalism, which the Man of Steel believes seeks to enslave the workers. Even the famous Superman insignia on the hero's chest has been altered to reflect Soviet society—the Superman emblem has been refashioned to include the Soviet symbol of the hammer and sickle.

Supervillains have taken the place of superheroes in some comic book stories. In one such story, a character named Nemesis uses his superpowers to hijack Air Force One (pictured) and take the president hostage.

Moreover, in many of his stories that feature numerous superheroes, such as Marvel's Avengers and Fantastic Four, Millar's plots usually find the characters in conflict. In one series, published by the Marvel subsidiary Icon, Millar's hero is no hero at all, but a supervillain: Nemesis. With illustrations by artist Steve McNiven, Nemesis finds no deed too cruel, no act too barbarous. He uses his superpowers to rob, murder, and commit sexual assault. In one episode, Nemesis hijacks Air Force One and takes the president hostage. In commenting on Millar's work, *New Republic* magazine critic Abraham Riesman says:

Throughout the '00s, he wrote some of Marvel's best-selling stories and radically reinvented characters such as the X-Men, Captain America, and Nick Fury. For example, Nick Fury—Marvel's premier superspy—had been depicted as a white grizzled World War II vet for decades; but Millar transformed him into a young, black, smooth-talking Gulf War hero. . . . Millar soon became a fan favorite in the Marvel stable, praised for meshing the dark satire of his earlier work with the technicolor wonder of the Marvel universe.[29]

Blurring the Line

The work of artists and writers such as Miller, Moore, Lee, Yu, and Millar illustrates how comic books have changed in recent years. The stories and artwork are produced for a more mature audience, reflecting the fact that comic books hold considerable appeal for adult readers. Certainly, comic books still feature enough action, superheroes, and thugs to keep young readers coming back for more, but those readers now find themselves challenged by the stories as they delve into topics where the line between good and evil is no longer clearly defined.

Chapter Four

Growth of the Graphic Novel

In 1986 DC Comics repackaged *Batman: The Dark Knight Returns* and *Watchmen* into book-length versions, each spanning hundreds of pages. Even though dedicated fans of the genre had already read the *Dark Knight* and *Watchmen* stories in their original comic book versions, both books sold well. It appeared that readers were developing an appetite for something more than the traditional thirty-two-page comic book.

These versions of *Dark Knight* and *Watchmen* are known in the book trade as graphic novels, a term first used by Will Eisner in 1978 to describe a book-length comic book–style story he wrote and illustrated titled *A Contract with God and Other Tenement Stories*. Starting in the 1930s, Eisner had been at the forefront of the movement to make the comic book into a home for superhero adventures. But *A Contract with God* featured no superhero adventures. Rather, the book, broken into four separate stories, focused on the plights of impoverished characters struggling through life in the tough tenement-filled neighborhoods of Depression-era New York City. In the initial story, the plot focuses on Frimme Hersh, a tycoon who owes his wealth to his hard-nosed business tactics but, near death, asks God for a second chance if he commits his life to philanthropy.

Although the book was set in an era many readers in the 1970s did not experience firsthand, Eisner believed little had changed in America some forty years after the Depression. Poor people still lived in tenement housing in US cities, and they still struggled to pay their bills, clothe their families, and put food on their tables. Therefore, Eisner believed the stories would find meaning among contemporary readers. In the preface to *A Contract with God* he writes, "It is important to understand the time and place in which these stories were set. Fundamentally, they were not unlike the way the world of today is for those who live in crowded proximity and in depersonalized housing. The importance of dealing with the ebb and flow of city existence and the overriding effort to escape it never seems to change for the inhabitants."[30]

A Lengthy Comic Book

Eisner's book spanned more than two hundred pages, meaning he had to maintain the sequential narrative far longer than the typical comic book reader was used to reading. Eisner had a lot of trouble convincing publishers to accept the manuscript—the concept of publishing a book-length comic book–style story was unknown in the American book business. Finally, though, Baronet Press, a small New York publisher, agreed to release the book.

A Contract with God did not sell well. Today book sales are largely driven by reader reviews posted on bookseller websites and social media. In the pre-Internet days, book sales were largely propelled by reviews published in major American newspapers and magazines, but book critics for those publications did not review comic books, and to them, *A Contract with God* was nothing more than a lengthy comic book. Moreover, few comic book stores were interested in carrying Eisner's

> **Words in Context**
> *manuscript*
> The initial draft of a book that authors show to publishers; if accepted for publication, the manuscript often undergoes extensive editing and revision.

Comic book artist Will Eisner (pictured at his drawing board in the 1990s) is considered a pioneer of graphic novels. When Eisner's book-length comic book–style story *A Contract with God* came out in 1978, bookstores had no idea what to do with it.

book in their inventory. After all, their clientele consisted largely of teenagers and young adults with a fascination for Spider-Man and Captain America. These were hardly the type of readers expected to browse through *A Contract with God*—unless they were assigned the book by their teachers. And teachers, at least in the 1970s, were not putting graphic novels on their assigned reading lists.

Even when *A Contract with God* was picked up by a mainstream bookstore, the store did not seem to know what to do with it. Soon after the book was published, Eisner learned that his graphic novel was being sold at Brentano's, a major New York City bookstore. Elated but not wanting to seem like an overeager author, Eisner waited two weeks before walking into the store to see how his book was being displayed. But after searching the store, he was unable to find the title. So Eisner sought out the manager and, after identifying himself as the author of *A Contract with God*, asked where he might find the book in the store.

The manager explained that at first, the book had been prominently displayed, but then the store had taken delivery on copies of a new novel by best-selling author James Michener and needed a place to display Michener's book, so Eisner's book was moved elsewhere. The manager told Eisner:

> I brought it inside and put it with the religious books since it's about God, and this little lady came up to me and said, "What's this book doing there? That's a cartoon book. It shouldn't be in with the religious books." So I took it out and put it in the humor section. . . . And someone came to me and said, "Hey, this isn't a funny book; there's nothing funny in this book. Why do you have it here?" I took it out of there and I didn't know where to put it.[31]

Stop-and-Start Reading

The Brentano's manager had, in fact, articulated a major roadblock to the establishment of the graphic novel as a legitimate form of literature and artistic expression. Graphic novels were not comic books—they were too long and lacked stories that focused on the plight of spandex-wearing superheroes. But they also did not fit into most people's concept of books, either. *New Yorker* magazine art critic Peter Schjeldahl explains the key problem: People who read books never take their eyes off the words, but people who read comic books must constantly read the words, then before moving on to the next panel, pause to absorb the art that accompanies the words.

Wendy Pini, Creator of *Elfquest*

Wendy Pini began her career in 1974 drawing illustrations for pulps such as the science-fiction magazines *Galaxy* and *Worlds of If*. The first comic book she illustrated was a title in the *Red Sonja* series for Marvel. She has also illustrated titles for DC Comics as well as some independent publishers, among them Comico and First Comics.

In 1978 Pini and her husband, Richard, founded WaRP Graphics as a vehicle to publish Pini's *Elfquest* comic book series, leading to the first *Elfquest* graphic novel in 1981. Since then Pini has written and illustrated several other graphic novels, among them a version of horror writer Edgar Allan Poe's *Masque of the Red Death* as well as a version of the fairy tale *Beauty and the Beast*.

Elfquest continues to enjoy a wide fan base. Pini says her inspiration for *Elfquest* can be found in Japanese manga, which focuses more on figures from fantasy—magicians, elves, fairies, and mythical warriors—than on superheroes. Moreover, Pini says, *Elfquest* made its debut as the *Star Wars* movies gained popularity in American culture, indicating that Americans were ready for stories of a fantastical nature. She says, "All of this was about timing. The stars had aligned. The American public was ready for a big, high-fantasy adventure. They were eating up *Star Wars* right then, and so they were looking for these big fantasy adventures, and we just happened to be able to supply one."

Quoted in Patrick A. Reed, "Timeless Fantasy and Indie Innovation: Wendy & Richard Pini on 36 Years of 'Elfquest,'" Comics Alliance, August 8, 2014. http://comics alliance.com.

Comic book readers may be willing to dedicate themselves to that process for a few dozen pages, but at the dawn of the graphic novel era, many publishers were skeptical that readers would endure that stop-and-start style of reading for books spanning a few hundred pages. Moreover, because comic books are short, most readers devour them start to finish in one sitting. Publishers wondered whether readers would accept the ritual of placing bookmarks between the pages of their graphic novels—essentially, stopping the action between one panel and the next—then picking up the story later. Says Schjeldahl, "Consuming them—toggling for hours between the incommensurable functions of reading and looking—is taxing. The difficulty of graphic novels limits their potential audience."[32]

> **Words in Context**
> *plot twist*
> A sudden and unexpected change in the direction of a story; usually, authors spend considerable effort setting up the plot twist so that it arrives unexpectedly and stuns the readers.

Defenders of graphic novels counter, though, that the typical comic book—because it spans no more than a few dozen pages—limits the writer and artist to a very basic story that pays little attention to the development of characters or to providing opportunity for plot twists. Although comic books had come a long way since the days of Joe Shuster and Jerry Siegel, with stories involving characters wrestling with their inner demons merged with art that reflected expressionism, the stories were nevertheless largely limited to simple plots.

High-Quality Reproduction

Now, though, artists and writers could spend hundreds of pages plotting out stories, taking readers into unexpected directions. Moreover, several pages could be devoted to examining the characters of the protagonists and the other individuals found in the stories. "Put simply, in a longer narrative there was more scope for building up tension, generating atmosphere, developing characters, and so on," says Roger Sabin. "At the same time, the visuals could often be superior to the usual comics, because the status of the work was supposedly higher."[33] Indeed, because book publishers typically use higher grades of paper than what is ordinarily found in comic book production, the art reproduces much better, meaning the physical and visual quality of the graphic novel is much better. It was a factor bound to attract

Experimental Graphic Novels

Writers and artists are using new techniques to produce graphic novels that go beyond merging words with pictures. For example, in 2011 writer Warren Ellis and artist Matt Brooker collaborated on a graphic novel detective story titled *SVK*. The book contains panels and dialogue similar to any other graphic novel, but it is sold with a pen that shines an ultraviolet light. When the pen is directed at the panels, it reveals balloons containing the hidden thoughts of the characters.

In 2010 the Museum of Contemporary Art and Redmoon Theater in Chicago collaborated on a graphic novel titled *The Astronaut's Birthday* that was not published on paper or in digital format but projected onto the front windows of the museum. The three rows of museum windows provided an 80-foot-tall (24 m) screen. Sitting on bleachers in front of the museum, readers followed the science-fiction story as it was projected by eighteen old-style overhead projectors.

And in 2013 artist Philipp Meyer, working with Nota, a Danish organization that produces audiobooks and books in Braille for the blind, published a graphic novel titled *Life*. The novel is illustrated in a series of raised dots that can be read by sight-impaired people. *Life* explores topics such as birth, love, procreation, and death. Says Meyer, "One has to take into consideration that most born-blind readers didn't get in contact with the comic medium ever before. My goal was to create a story that is equally explorable for people with and without eyesight."

Quoted in Alison Nastasi, "A Brief Survey of Experimental Comic Books," Flavorwire, June 15, 2013. http://flavorwire.com.

comic book artists to the new genre, given their frustration with the low quality of reproduction of their work found in comic books even with offset printing.

Despite the limited success of *A Contract with God*, and despite the questions raised by publishers about the desire of readers to remain with a sequential narrative for hundreds of pages, other artists and writers started producing graphic novels soon after Eisner's title was released. As with *A Contract with God*, these titles did not focus on the adventures of superheroes but rather on poignant stories that spoke to human frailties and fears. In 1978 the British artist Raymond Briggs published *The Snowman*, a fairy tale in graphic novel form—albeit without dialogue—that tells the story of a boy who builds and befriends a snowman. Three years later he told a much darker story in *When the Wind Blows*, which examines the harsh reality of nuclear war.

Inner Conflict

In the meantime, a major breakthrough occurred in 1979 when Jules Feiffer, a popular magazine cartoonist, published the graphic novel *Tantrum*. Even though Eisner and Briggs were well-respected writers and illustrators, their names lacked the heft of Feiffer's, who had a large international following of dedicated readers. *Tantrum* is a tale geared toward a mature audience. The plot centers on Leo, a middle-aged man who discovers the ability to return to childhood. As a child, though, Leo retains the knowledge and sense of responsibility he knew as an adult. Therefore, the story tells of the inner conflict Leo faces as he tries to live life as a young boy but is constantly weighed down with the emotions that burden a much older man. Says Stephen Weiner, director of the Maynard Public Library in Massachusetts and a well-known comic book historian, "*Tantrum* was a striking departure for the cartoonist. Not only were the themes expressed in *Tantrum* startling, the drawings were bold. The illustrations possessed a kind of electricity which allowed them to open into each other almost breathlessly. The combination of the tortured theme and the magnetic drawings made for compelling reading."[34]

The graphic novels by Eisner, Briggs, and Feiffer aimed for readers who would not otherwise be expected to be fans of comic books. But the two genres found a way to merge in 1981 when artist and writer Wendy Pini published a graphic novel using the characters from an existing comic book series titled *Elfquest*. The series, launched in 1976 by WaRP Graphics, an independent publisher started by Pini and her husband, Richard, had earned a dedicated following of readers. By the early 1980s each *Elfquest* issue sold about one hundred thousand copies.

The series tells the story of a race of elves in search of their homeland. Moreover, Pini filled the stories with strong female characters. In *Elfquest*, the females are more than just sexy villains or women in distress—they are archers, hunters, athletes, warriors, and leaders. Therefore, *Elfquest* is one of the few comic book series that found a strong readership among girls and young women. And so in 1981, when WaRP Graphics published the first *Elfquest* graphic novel— and it racked up respectable sales—mainstream book publishers concluded that girls and young women were willing to buy graphic novels. The likelihood of strong sales among female readers was an important factor in convincing major book publishers to start producing graphic novels.

Breakout Title

The breakout title that established the graphic novel as an important source of literature and art in popular culture was *Maus: A Survivor's Tale*. The first volume of the two-volume set was released in 1986. Written and illustrated by Art Spiegelman, *Maus* tells the story of the Holocaust, during which millions of Europeans, mostly Jews, were rounded up by the Nazi regime in Germany and imprisoned in concentration camps. Spiegelman's parents were concentration camp survivors. He sought to tell their story through the eyes of comic book characters while also using the story to explain the troubled relationship he had with his father in the years following his parents' liberation from a concentration camp at the end of World War II.

Maus had, in fact, been published six years prior to its release as a graphic novel. Starting in 1980, Spiegelman published episodes from the story in a little-known magazine titled *Raw*. The 1986 graphic novel version—released by Pantheon, a major American publishing house—consisted mostly of reprints of the original *Raw* episodes.

In Spiegelman's story Jews are portrayed as mice and German

Art Spiegelman's *Maus: A Survivor's Tale* established the graphic novel as an important form of both art and literature. The two-volume work depicts Jews as mice and Nazis as cats to tell the story of the millions who were imprisoned (pictured) and killed during the Holocaust.

soldiers are illustrated as cats. Artist and comic book historian Robert C. Harvey says Spiegelman's decision to tell the story through the eyes of mice and cats illustrates the nature of the "cat-and-mouse" game that was very much a part of the Holocaust. He says, "Depicting the Jews as mice and the Nazis as cats immediately established the 'cat-and-mouse' game as the books' overarching thematic image—and the expression has an unfortunate resonance," he says. "As anyone who has watched a cat toy with a mouse knows, the 'game' has a . . . grisly outcome."[35] Therefore, Harvey says, Spiegelman's decision to use cats and mice in the story shows how the Nazis toyed with the Jews, falsely promising them humane treatment or permission to leave Germany when the Nazis' intentions were evil all along.

Maus was an enormously popular book, earning a place on the *New York Times* best-seller list. But *Maus* was much more than a commercial success: In 1992 Spiegelman was awarded a Pulitzer Prize, regarded as the nation's highest honor for journalism, literature, and drama.

Graphic Novels in the Classroom

Maus helped establish the legitimacy of the graphic novel not only among readers but among educators as well. In 2014 the *School Library Journal* reported, "Because the last decade has seen a sharp increase in the number and quality of graphic novels published for readers of all ages, they are more common in classrooms and school libraries. Publishers often provide lesson plans [and] information on curricula."[36]

Moreover, even graphic novels that focus on the exploits of superheroes or other fantastic stories can be useful in the classroom. The *School Library Journal* cited the example of the Zombie-Based Learning program, which produces graphic novels that teach lessons in all manner of subjects—from social studies to vocabulary—by using zombies to illustrate the stories. "In sixth-grade teacher Jennifer DeFeo's social studies class at Thomas Jefferson Middle School in Jefferson City, Missouri, the textbook is a graphic novel, the centerpiece of the Zombie-Based Learning program, in which students learn geography by tracking the undead after a zombie apocalypse," reported the *School Library Journal*. "She has used graphic novels in literacy classes to build vocabulary . . . which can be hard for some readers using prose books."[37]

Graphic Nonfiction

As graphic novels became more popular, publishers added a new type of illustrated story to their inventories: graphic nonfiction. A typical example is *The Stuff of Life*, which explains genetic science through the use of words and illustrations. The book uses a comic book format that looks as if it fell off the pages of a Batman or Superman adventure. Written by Mark Schultz and illustrated by Zander Cannon and Kevin Cannon, *The Stuff of Life* tells the story of the chemical properties of cells and how they combine to form life.

To produce the 2009 book, the publisher called on the talents of professionals from the comic book industry. Schultz has written Superman stories as well as titles in many other superhero series for a number of publishers, and the Cannons are veteran comic book illustrators. To tell the story, the author and the artists give voices to single-celled organisms, who relate the science to the readers. Says Schultz:

> *The Stuff of Life* is a science primer—a high school level introduction to the science of genetics—told in a comics format. To get across the sometimes incredibly complex information needed to understand the subject, it employs a fictional problem-solving framework. . . . We look at the mechanics of genetics—from the molecular workings of DNA up through the rules of heredity, and then at how mankind is applying his growing knowledge of the subjects in a practical—and sometimes impractical—manner. I know it sounds dry, and it is admittedly dense material, but it is [a] fascinating and incredibly relevant subject that will have a growing and unavoidable impact on all our lives.[38]

Rising Popularity

Titles such as *Maus* and *A Contract with God* suggest that although superheroes can certainly be found in the pages of graphic novels, the books offer opportunities for writers and artists to explore real-world dramas using the techniques of sequential art. And given the rising popularity of graphic novels and graphic nonfiction as well as their acceptance by educators, readers now have little trouble finding them on the racks of American bookstores.

Chapter Five

Comic Book Art in the Digital Age

Dedicated comic book readers look forward to Wednesdays. That is the day each week when Marvel, DC, and smaller publishers release their latest titles. Owners of comic book stores know Wednesdays are their busiest days, since eager readers flock to their stores to buy the latest episodes chronicling the adventures of their favorite superheroes.

Readers who buy their comic books in digital versions also have to wait until Wednesdays for their releases to be made available. When they download and open their digital editions, computer, tablet, and smartphone readers often find a much different experience than print readers find in their versions.

Many digital comic books include music and sound effects that accompany the text and images. In some digital comic books, the artwork may be animated to a minor degree. Some digital comic books are even interactive. For example, an application developed for Apple devices enables users to play a video game when they reach the conclusion of the *Batman* episode they have downloaded. "[The app takes] advantage of the interactive elements of the device," says Hank Kanalz, senior vice president of interactive publishing for DC. "This is all touch screen. You control the pace of how you read it."[39]

Ben Wolstenholme, chief executive officer of Madefire (the company that designed the app), says the abilities of tablets, smartphones and computers to display more than just text and illustrations has brought new challenges for comic book publishers. "We have supercomputers in our pockets; we should expect more than just [a comic book] scanned in print."[40]

The Digital Revolution

Marvel also provides an app for its readers. Since 2014 the company has included codes in the pages of the print versions of its comic books. By using a Marvel app installed on their smartphones or tablets, readers can pass their screens over the codes, opening extra features on their devices, such as animations of the characters. "We view it as the new, newsstand to find new fans," says Axel Alonso, Marvel

The First Digitally Created Comic Book

The first comic book produced with computer tools was an issue in the series *Shatter*, which told of a future society in which the intelligence and skills of the brightest citizens are stolen by sapping out their genetic material. (Shatter is the name of the hero, a tough cop who discovers the plan.) Written by Peter B. Gillis and illustrated by artist Mike Saenz, the first issue made its debut in 1985.

Saenz produced all of the story's artwork using an Apple Macintosh computer and an early version of graphic design software known as MacPaint. The artwork was rendered in black and white and then printed on a dot matrix printer, which created images by producing them in a series of tiny black dots. Finally, Saenz colored the pages the old-fashioned way—with ink and paint.

Shatter was produced by a small independent publisher, First Comics. The first Marvel title created on a computer screen was *Iron Man: Crash* in 1988. DC Comics produced its first digitally created title in 1990 when it published *Batman: Digital Justice*.

editor in chief. "By moving into the digital arena, [we can] take advantage of the technology and tools to continue telling a comic book story . . . just on a different platform."[41]

Online versions of comic books date back to 1997, when Marvel published online editions of Spider-Man and Wolverine adventures. These comic books were strictly available online—they could not be downloaded onto a computer and read offline. Moreover, Marvel released the comic books in partnership with AOL—then known as America Online. At the time, AOL was a subscription-based service—members had to pay a monthly fee to access its website. Therefore, only AOL members could read Marvel's digital comic books.

To view the online comic book, a reader moved from panel to panel with mouse clicks. Marvel did add some extra features to the online versions, such as animating some of the panels. In 1998 Marvel created its own website, making online comic books available to all readers. DC also established a website that year featuring digital content.

> **Words in Context**
> *pixels*
> Tiny points of illumination drawn together on a computer screen to form shapes; pixels compose both digital illustrations and photographs.

By then publishers had been making novels and other popular books available in e-book formats that could be downloaded onto desktop and laptop computers—tablets and smartphones would not be developed and marketed widely until the 2000s. However, a number of manufacturers developed e-readers: handheld devices devoted specifically to displaying digital versions of books. Comic book publishers were slow to embrace the new technology. DC did not start releasing e-book versions of its titles until 2010. Marvel first released an e-book version of a Spider-Man adventure in 2011.

Comic book publishers resisted making their titles into digital versions, fearing a loss in print sales. However, as more and more consumers demanded digital versions, the publishers finally relented and started making their titles available in e-book formats. Reported *Publishers Weekly* in 2013, "There are essentially no longer any holdouts—even smaller more art-focused publishers are getting on the digital bandwagon. Many had resisted, fearing lost print sales and a loss of quality, but many of their own artists began to clamor for it."[42]

Convergence of Pixels

It is easy to see why comic book artists pressured their publishers to offer digital versions. The stark and colorful artwork found in comic books and graphic novels reproduces much better in digital format than on paper. Even with the techniques available in modern offset printing and the high-quality paper used in graphic novels, comic book art nevertheless loses resolution when ink is absorbed by paper during the printing process. "Comics, as it happens, look magnificent on tablets,"[43] says Douglas Wolk, an author and expert on the comic book industry. Now publishers routinely release both print and digital versions of new titles, and both DC and Marvel have reproduced large selections from their archives, dating back decades, as e-books.

The images on the screen are actually the convergence of pixels, the minute points of illumination that are gathered together by the computer to form shapes. The more pixels that are concentrated in an image, the higher the resolution. Most digital art ranges from seventy-two pixels per inch to three hundred pixels per inch.

The digitization of comic book art owes much of its development to the revolution in software that made comic book artists largely reliant on their computers to create their illustrations. Starting in the 1990s, artists found a new set of tools, thanks to the development of programs such as Adobe Photoshop, Adobe Illustrator, Manga Studio, and Corel Painter.

Tablet and Stylus

Practically speaking, most artists begin with rough sketches made with pencil and paper. These sketches are then digitized—scanned using technology that dates back to the 1970s. The scanning process was developed in 1976 by engineer Ray Kurzweil, who invented the technology known as optical character recognition. To digitize a pencil sketch, an artist places the page facedown on the glass surface of a

A digital artist demonstrates the technique of using a stylus on a large tablet to draw a character. Most comic book artists who use digital technology scan their rough sketches into a computer and then use the stylus to make changes and fine-tune their drawings.

flatbed scanner. Beneath the glass, a light-sensitive element known as a charge-coupled device (CCD) illuminates the page, recording the information that comes into contact with the light. The image is then transferred to a computer, which accepts the data from the CCD and converts it into an image on a screen.

In the typical digital artist's studio of the twenty-first century, the computer screen is not sitting vertically behind a keyboard but, rather, is found lying flat on the desk as a tablet. Moreover, the tablets used by professional artists are much larger than the typical iPads or Kindle Fires. Wacom, a leading manufacturer of artists' tablets, produces devices that are as large as 21 inches (53 cm) square, giving the artist 441 square inches (2,845 sq. cm) of space on which to work.

The artist works on the tablet with a stylus—an electronic pen than can draw directly on the tablet surface. The pen does not leave behind a trail of ink but, rather, a trail of electrical impulses that create lines and shapes—whatever the artist chooses to draw. Although original images can be created with a stylus, most comic book artists use the stylus to alter the rough pencil sketches that have already been scanned into the computer.

Resize, Rotate, and Nudge

As for what can be drawn with a stylus and tablet surface compared to what can be accomplished with pencil and paper, the artist is limited only by his or her talents and imagination. Says British comic book artist Brian Bolland:

> I work entirely in Adobe Photoshop. . . . There are lots of nifty things you can do in Photoshop that you can't do with pen and ink. You can enlarge the image or flip it. You can paint a lighter color over a darker color, and you never have to clear your brush or buy a new one. You have a special tool that allows you to draw curves. You can lasso bits of your drawing and move them about or change the size and, at a stroke, you can undo any mistake you make. . . . I've never managed to find the button that gets the computer to draw the picture for me, so when the page is finished I can honestly say that it was done by my own fair hand and not "computer generated."[44]

The Future of the Comic Book Store

Back in the 1950s and 1960s, music fans bought their music at stores that sold vinyl records, and many stores offered private booths where customers could listen to sample tracks before deciding whether to purchase the records. Moreover, many fans relied on the expertise of the clerks, who steered them toward hot new recording artists. Few such record stores exist today; most have been replaced by music downloaded from online vendors in MP3 format.

As more and more comic books become available in digital formats, many industry insiders fear the comic book stores may go into virtual extinction—as the record stores have. They worry that such changes will dilute the experience. Archie Comics president Mike Pellerito says there has long been a social aspect of readers going to comic book stores, browsing through titles, and relying on the advice of the clerks. That degree of interaction is not a part of downloading a digital comic book from a website, he says.

David Steinberger, chief executive officer of Comi-Xology, a top vendor of digital comic books, counters that publishers as well as digital vendors are dedicated to preserving print versions. Steinberger says ComiXology provides a service in its digital versions that advises readers where to find comic book stores in their communities. He says, "We have a store finder in the [ComiXology] app. At the end of every comic, there's a little 'buy in print' button so you can see where a local store is. And hopefully, we'll continue to drive people there as well."

Quoted in Vaneta Rogers, "Will Digital Kill the Comic Book Store?," Newsarama, August 10, 2011. www.newsarama.com.

Freddie E. Williams II, a writer and artist who has illustrated the Flash and a series featuring Robin, Batman's teenage sidekick, embraced digital technology early in his career. Creating a comic book panel on paper, he says, may require the artist to rough out several sketches of the scene before deciding which sketch to take into the further stages of development, resulting in the finished, full-color panel. Williams says a single rough sketch can be scanned into the computer and then, by using a stylus and tablet, altered many times until the artist is satisfied with the configuration of the elements in the scene.

Moreover, he says, each version of the sketch can be saved so that the artist can constantly copy elements from one sketch and move them into another. "Have you ever drawn a hand or head and then noticed that it's too large or just a bit off kilter?" he asks. "On paper, you have to erase and redraw—and I find that the redrawn element almost never seems as good as the original. But when you are working in the digital world, you can simply isolate that head or hand and then resize, rotate, nudge, or distort it until it feels right."[45]

Altering Chest Symbols

In addition to giving the artist wide latitude to make changes, using programs like Adobe Photoshop can be a great time-saver. Williams says that when he has to draw a building, he never starts by making a pencil sketch. Instead, he takes a digital photo of a building and then, using the features of the software, converts the photo into an image that resembles a hand-drawn sketch. Finally, he adds colors to the building that reflects the style in which the panel is rendered.

Williams does not use the same techniques to draw characters. But certain elements of his comic book characters are easily transferrable from one image to the next. Specifically, Williams says he can save a lot of time by using the same version of the superhero chest symbol over and over again. Many superheroes sport familiar symbols on their chests. For Superman, it is a large *S* contained within a geometric shape that resembles an upside-down triangle. Batman's chest symbol is the image of a black bat, its wings spread wide, inside a

Words in Context

stylus
A device resembling a pen that can draw on a tablet screen, forming images through electrical impulses.

Software programs like Adobe Photoshop can save artists a lot of time, especially for repetitive tasks like drawing familiar superhero symbols such as this one used for Batman. This leaves the artist more time to draw the characters.

yellow oval. The Flash wears a symbol that features a yellow lightning bolt laid over a white circle. By using Adobe Photoshop, Williams says, he can turn, curve, and distort the symbol to suit the posture of the character, then lay it into the panel. "As you do this, you're warping the path, rounding it to fit snugly on the chest of our hero,"[46] he says.

Is It Art?

Artists like Williams and Bolland use the stylus and tablet to produce the same type of artwork that was produced a generation ago by artists who worked solely on paper and made their images using pencils, pens, and brushes. The most significant difference, though, in the production of comic book art today is the addition of the computer to assist the artist. And because the computer has become an integral tool in the production of a comic book illustration, artists like Bolland and Williams hear criticisms similar to the criticisms first heard by Shuster, Eisner, and similar artists of their generation: Is comic book art really art? Says Sean Frank, a London art gallery owner, "There's a lot of debate asking, 'Is [digital art] an art form?' It's just so subjective. Some people will never think it is."[47]

Digital artists defend their craft. "Great debate rages about using computers to create art," says writer and illustrator Ron Miller. "People have asked questions such as 'Is digital art real art?' or 'Is digital art cheating?' These questions have led to some heated discussions."[48] Miller argues that over the course of hundreds of years, as artistic techniques evolved, new tools were constantly introduced to the artists. Over the centuries, oil paints were introduced, giving portrait and landscape painters vivid colors to use in their work. Acrylic paints—which dry faster than oils and watercolors—were not developed until the 1940s. A faster-drying paint proved to be a great time-saver for many artists, who could add details to surfaces that had already been painted without waiting hours for the oils or watercolors to dry. Photography has long been regarded as an art form, but photography was not invented until the nineteenth century—hundreds of years after painters started making images on canvas. And by the 1990s, digital imaging had replaced film as the primary medium used in photography—saving photographers hours of labor in their darkrooms.

Thrills and Adventure

Miller and other artists argue that the equipment available to artists today—the tablet, stylus, and software—are no more than new tools that enable artists to make art. Indeed, proponents of digital art contend, somebody equipped with all the high-tech tools available could not create a believable image of Batman if that person lacks the talent, imagination, and training of a true artist. Says Dutch illustrator Jan Willem Wennekes:

> I think that working with digital media (mostly the computer, mouse, Wacom, scanner, software, etc.) does not have to differ from creating art in other media. The computer and all the tools generated by the software are still what they are: tools! You have to master those tools just as you have to master any

other tools. For example, if you do not understand how light works, you won't be able to create artwork with correct lighting, and so on. If you don't know how the pen tool works in [Adobe] Illustrator, then you won't be able to create good

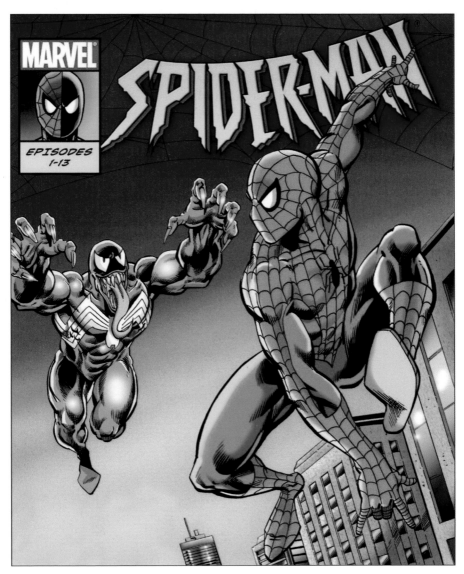

For as long as comic books have been around, artists have heard this question: Is comic book art really art? The answer would seem to be a resounding yes.

artwork, just like a traditional artist who doesn't know how to use a pencil. You still have to master color theory and all the other things that are essential to creating a good or stunning piece of art. In that sense, it doesn't matter whether it is a painting or a print. Simply put, you have to master all the tools and theory, just as you had to master them before. And the better you master them, the better your artwork can be.[49]

Whether comic book art is created entirely with pencil, pen, and paintbrush or entirely with a stylus and screen—or with a combination of the two sets of tools—the outcome is the same: a vivid and stirring image of a costumed superhero in the midst of a grand adventure. The techniques of creating this art may have changed over the years, but the comic book remains an important source of thrills for millions of readers.

Source Notes

Introduction: The Enduring Art of the Comic Book

1. Scott Foundas, "Film Review: *Avengers: Age of Ultron*," *Variety*, April 21, 2015. http://variety.com.
2. Roger Sabin, *Comics, Comix & Graphic Novels: A History of Comic Art*. London: Phaidon, 2014, p. 8.
3. Gus Lubin, "The Comic Book Industry Is On Fire, and It's About More than Just the Movies," Business Insider, August 24, 2014. www.businessinsider.com.
4. Quoted in Caroline A. Miranda, "The Boundary Between Fine Art and Graphic Novels Has Grown Increasingly Porous," *ARTnews*, October 11, 2011. www.artnews.com.
5. Quoted in Miranda, "The Boundary Between Fine Art and Graphic Novels Has Grown Increasingly Porous."

Chapter One: The Art of Telling Stories

6. Norman Cousins, "Not So Fast," *Educational Leadership*, December 1963, pp. 145–46.
7. Sabin, *Comics, Comix & Graphic Novels*, p. 9.
8. Will Eisner, *Comics and Sequential Art: Principles and Practices from the Legendary Cartoonist*. New York: Norton, 2008, p. 127.
9. Robert C. Harvey, *The Art of the Comic Book: An Aesthetic History*. Jackson: University Press of Mississippi, 1996, p. 10.
10. Eisner, *Comics and Sequential Art*, p. 90.
11. Joseph Witek, "The Arrow and the Grid," in Jeet Heer and Kent Worcester, eds., *A Comics Studies Reader*. Jackson: University Press of Mississippi, 2009, p. 153.
12. Sam Adams, Noel Murray, Keith Phipps, and Leonard Pierce, "Reinventing the Pencil: 21 Artists Who Changed Mainstream Comics (for Better or Worse)," A.V. Club, July 20, 2009. www.avclub.com.
13. Adams et al., "Reinventing the Pencil."

14. Quoted in Jeff McLaughlin, ed., *Stan Lee: Conversations*. Jackson: University Press of Mississippi, 2007, p. 164.
15. Eisner, *Comics and Sequential Art*, p. 132.
16. Eisner, *Comics and Sequential Art*, p. 24.

Chapter Two: Conquest of the Superheroes

17. Joe Simon, *My Life in Comics*. London: Titan, 2011, p. 87.
18. Sabin, *Comics, Comix & Graphic Novels*, p. 62.
19. Harvey, *The Art of the Comic Book*, p. 35.
20. Quoted in Deborah Friedell, "Kryptonomics," *New Yorker*, June 24, 2013, p. 80.
21. Quoted in Les Daniels, *Superman: The Complete History*. San Francisco: Chronicle, 1998, p. 17.
22. Friedell, "Kryptonomics," p. 80.
23. Jordan Raphael and Tom Spurgeon, *Stan Lee and the Rise and Fall of the American Comic Book*. Chicago: Chicago Review, 2003, p. 87.
24. Quoted in William B. Jones Jr., *Classics Illustrated: A Cultural History*. Jefferson, NC: McFarland, 2011, p. 4.

Chapter Three: Comic Books Enter the Dark Side

25. Maggie Gray, "Saga of the Swamp Thing," in Paul Gravett, ed., *1001 Comics You Must Read Before You Die: The Ultimate Guide to Comic Books, Graphic Novels, and Manga*. New York: Universe, 2011, p. 467.
26. Christopher Irving, "Frank Miller Part 1: Dames, *Dark Knight*s, Devils, and Heroes," Graphic NYC, December 1, 2010. www.nycgraphicnovelists.com.
27. Sabin, *Comics, Comix & Graphic Novels*, p. 162.
28. Marc-Oliver Frisch, "Jim Lee," in M. Keith Booker, ed., *Encyclopedia of Comics and Graphic Novels*. Santa Barbara, CA: ABC-CLIO, 2010, p. 362.
29. Abraham Riesman, "'You're Done Banging Superheroes, Baby,' How the Sickest Mind in Comic Books Became Their Biggest Star," *New Republic*, August 6, 2013. www.newrepublic.com.

Chapter Four: Growth of the Graphic Novel

30. Quoted in Jeremy Dauber, "Comic Books, Tragic Stories: Will Eisner's American Jewish History," in Samantha Baskind and Ranen Omer-Sherman, eds., *The Jewish Graphic Novel: Critical Approaches*. Piscat-

away, NJ: Rutgers University Press, 2008, pp. 27–28.

31. Quoted in Michael Schumacher, *Will Eisner: A Dreamer's Life in Comics*. New York: Bloomsbury, 2010, p. 205.

32. Peter Schjeldahl, "Graphic Novels Come of Age," *New Yorker*, October 17, 2005. www.newyorker.com.

33. Sabin, *Comics, Comix & Graphic Novels*, p. 165.

34. Stephen Weiner, *Faster than a Speeding Bullet: The Rise of the Graphic Novel*. New York: Nantier Ball Minoustchine, 2003, p. 23.

35. Harvey, *The Art of the Comic Book*, p. 35.

36. Brigid Alverson, "Teaching with Graphic Novels," *School Library Journal*, September 8, 2014. www.slj.com.

37. Alverson, "Teaching with Graphic Novels."

38. Quoted in Flesk Publications, "Mark Schultz *Stuff of Life* Interview," 2009. www.fleskpublications.com.

Chapter Five: Comic Book Art in the Digital Age

39. Quoted in Marc Graser, "DC Entertainment Turns Video Games into Interactive Comic Books," *Variety*, December 19, 2013. http://variety.com.

40. Quoted in Graser, "DC Entertainment Turns Video Games into Interactive Comic Books."

41. Quoted in Bigad Shaban, "The Evolution of Comic Books in the Digital Age," CBS News, July 22, 2014. www.cbsnews.com.

42. Bruce Lidl, "Digital Comics: Adding Readers and Flexibility," *Publishers Weekly*, August 14, 2013. www.publishersweekly.com.

43. Douglas Wolk, "The iPad Could Revolutionize the Comic Book Biz—or Destroy It," *Wired*, June 25, 2011. www.wired.com.

44. Brian Bolland, foreword to *The DC Guide to Drawing Digital Comics*, by Freddie E. Williams II. New York: Watson-Guptill, 2009, p. 5.

45. Williams, *The DC Guide to Drawing Digital Comics*, p. 15.

46. Williams, *The DC Guide to Drawing Digital Comics*, p. 99.

47. Sean Frank and Margot Bowman, "Can Digital Art Be Called Art?," British Council, February 27, 2015. www.britishcouncil.org.

48. Ron Miller, *Digital Art: Painting with Pixels*. Minneapolis, MN: Twenty-First Century, 2008, p. 4.

49. Quoted in Marilina Maraviglia, "What Do We Mean by Art?," *Smashing Magazine*, July 3, 2010. www.smashingmagazine.com.

For Further Research

Books

Sean Howe, *Marvel Comics: The Untold Story*. New York: Harper-Perennial, 2013.

Jill Lepore, *The Secret History of Wonder Woman*. New York: Vintage, 2015.

John Paul Lowe, *Foundations in Comic Book Art: Fundamental Tools and Techniques for Sequential Artists*. New York: Crown, 2014.

Carl Potts, *The DC Comics Guide to Creating Comics: Inside the Art of Visual Storytelling*. New York: Crown, 2013.

Roger Sabin, *Comics, Comix & Graphic Novels: A History of Comic Art*. London: Phaidon, 2014.

Websites

Cartoon Art Museum (http://cartoonart.org). The San Francisco–based Cartoon Art Museum is dedicated to exhibiting examples of cartoon art, including comic books and graphic novels. The website features information about many of the museum's exhibitions, such as displays of costumes from films featuring superheroes, as well as the work of little-known artists who provide illustrations for independent comic publishers.

Comichron: The Comics Chronicles (www.comichron.com). Comichron examines the business side of the comic book industry, posting sales figures for comic books by month and year, dating back to the 1960s. Also, the sales for the top three hundred comics per decade are reported. A time line provides a brief history of the comic book industry.

Comics Alliance (http://comicsalliance.com). Comic book fans can find many essays by experts examining the trends in comic book publishing, including criticisms of the quality of art and writing found in contemporary comic books. The website covers a thorough history of comic book art; under the link for "Art," for example, readers can follow the evolution of the design for Wonder Woman.

Crumb Museum (www.zubeworld.com/crumbmuseum). The website features an online museum dedicated to the work of underground comic book artist Robert Crumb. Visitors can find many covers of *Zap Comix*. By following the link for "Character Gallery," visitors can see a selection of Crumb's art, including images of his best-known character, Fritz the Cat.

Digital Arts (www.digitalartsonline.co.uk). The British-based website provides information on the latest developments in digital art. Visitors can access videos of artists creating digital art with the stylus and tablet. Also, the website provides tutorials on using Adobe Photoshop and other software to create digital art.

Expressionism, Guggenheim (www.guggenheim.org/new-york/col lections/collection-online/movements/195214). Sponsored by the New York City–based Guggenheim Museum, the website provides an overview of expressionism, the movement that has dominated comic book art since the 1980s. Visitors to the site can see the work of early twentieth-century expressionists such as Vasily Kandinsky, Lyonel Feininger, Max Beckmann, and Max Ernst.

Inheritance (www.pbs.org/pov/inheritance/photo_gallery_special_ maus.php#.VaJt-vlVikp). The companion website to the 2008 PBS documentary *Inheritance*, which focuses on the survivors of the Nazi Holocaust, features a video interview with Art Spiegelman. The artist and writer discusses the creation of his Pulitzer Prize–winning graphic novel, *Maus: A Survivor's Tale*.

Superheroes: A Never Ending Battle (www.pbs.org/superheroes). The companion website to the 2013 PBS television series *Superheroes: A Never Ending Battle* chronicles the emergence of the superhero on comic book pages as well as in other facets of popular culture. The website features interviews with former Marvel publisher Stan Lee and actress Lynda Carter, who portrayed Wonder Woman in a 1970s TV series.

Will Eisner (www.willeisner.com). The website is devoted to the work of the late Will Eisner, a leader in establishing the comic book as a form of sequential art. Visitors can read a biography of Eisner and see several examples of his work, including many covers from the adventures of the Spirit, the superhero he created.

Index

Picture Credits

Hal Marcovitz is a former newspaper reporter and columnist who has written nearly two hundred books for young readers. He makes his home in Chalfont, Pennsylvania.